APPETIZERS
APPETIZERS
APPETIZERS

DELICIOUS, EASY-TO-PREPARE STARTERS FOR ANY MEAL

JUDI OLSTEIN

Photographs by George G. Wieser

Distributed by Book Club of America
150 Motor Parkway
Hauppague, NY 11788
Tel: 516-434-1932
Fax: 516-434-4865

Produced by The Triangle Group, Ltd.
227 Park Avenue
Hoboken, NJ 07030

Design: Tony Meisel
Food styling and art direction: Brock Houghten
Special thanks to Broadway Panhandler and Margot Hughes
Origination and printing: Paramount Printing Group Ltd.

Printed in Hong Kong

ISBN 0-944297-07-2

Contents

Introduction

Every meal needs a beginning and too often it is pedestrian and unexciting. Appetizers should catch the eye, entice the nose and get the taste buds tingling. They should do all this without drowning out the flavors of the food to come.

In the days of multi-course meals and formal dinners, appetizers were reserved for lunch. Dinners started with soup, or so Escoffier commanded. Today's eaters can't be bothered with formal edicts about what to eat and when, but we can show some good taste in choosing foods that complement each other and tastes that don't clash.

Remember that a first course followed by a main course of similar ingredients will be, if nothing else, boring, unless the contrasts in flavor and texture are wide. Shellfish salad followed by red snapper with a spicy sauce makes sense; deviled eggs followed by an omelet does not.

Appetizers contains recipes for light yet satisfying first courses for everyday dinners and entertainments. A number of these dishes make good party food and can be multiplied to feed crowds.

Also, most of these dishes can be made in double quantities to serve as main courses for lunches and suppers. With the addition of a salad, some good, crusty bread and a glass of wine, they become perfect, quickly-made vehicles for entertaining and informal repasts.

The basic ingredients for appetizers are all readily available in most supermarkets—olive oil, fresh herbs, salad greens, tomatoes, sausages, olives, smoked fish and breads and crackers of every variety.

Combining these with meats, fish and vegetables to make stimulating starters is the aim of this book. But experimentation lies with you. Don't be afraid to create new combinations, to try new and unusual ingredients. Following are the foundations, the final touches are yours.

Left: An appetizing array of salad ingredients

Following pages: Smoked Fish, from the top—trout, salmon, mackerel

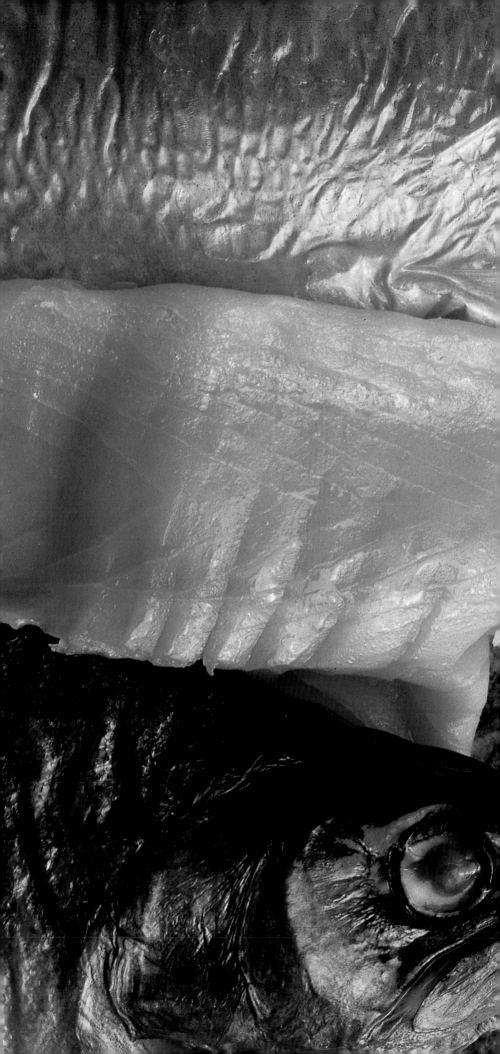

A selection of sausages
makes a hearty appetizer.

Breads and crackers are a perfect
accompaniment for appetizers.

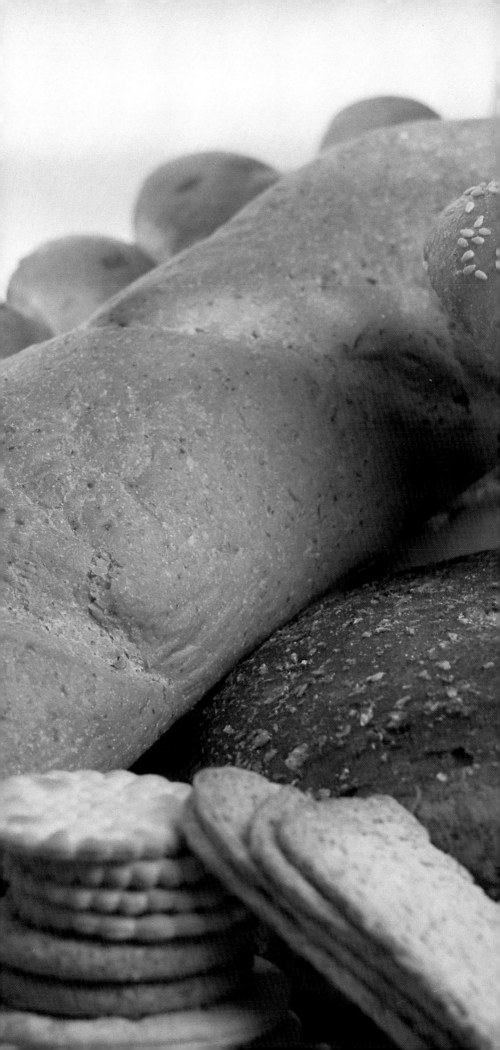

Cheese Log

An old favorite, but one that can be made far more interesting than is usually the case.

1 pound sharp cheddar
1/2 cup yogurt
1 tablespoon fresh sage, finely chopped
2 tablespoons Madeira or port
1 teaspoon freshly ground black pepper
1/2 cup walnuts, coarsely chopped

Grate the cheddar into a large mixing bowl. Add the yogurt, sage, Madeira or port and pepper and mix well (best done with a pair of clean hands). If the mixture is too stiff, add a bit more wine until a firm but pliable consistency is reached.

Roll the resultant mixture into a log shape, press into a mold or form into a loaf. Press the chopped walnuts over the surface and refrigerate for at least 4 hours. Let stand at room temperature for an hour before serving with crackers or rounds of crisp toast. Serves 6 as a single appetizer, 12 or more as part of a buffet.

Left: Cheese Log

Following pages: Shrimp Cocktail

Shrimp Cocktail

The bane of everyone's dinner party existence, a shrimp cocktail can be deeply satisfying if the shrimp are not overcooked and the sauce is not the red menace!

2 pounds large shrimp, shelled and deveined
1/2 cup dry white wine
1 teaspoon black peppercorns, roughly cracked
1 teaspoon salt
3/4 cup extra virgin olive oil
2 tablespoons wine vinegar
1 tablespoon grainy Dijon mustard
1 tablespoon fresh tarragon, finely chopped

Place the shrimp, white wine, peppercorns and salt in a saucepan with enough cold water to barely cover the ingredients. Bring to a boil, covered. Immediately remove from the heat and let stand 5 minutes. Drain the shrimp.

Combine the olive oil, vinegar, mustard and tarragon in a jar and shake well to blend.

Arrange the shrimp—at room temperature— on individual plates and pour the dressing into small dishes for dipping. Serves 6-8.

Oysters on the Half-Shell

Again, a strike against the red menace! If you like oysters, there's no need to disguise their flavor. If you don't like oysters, read on.

For each serving:
6 oysters on the half-shell
6 halves lemon

Arrange each half-dozen oysters on a bed of ice in a shallow soup plate. Add lemon halves.

For those who wish a dipping sauce:
Combine, for each serving, 1/4 cup dry white wine, 1 teaspoon wine vinegar, 1/4 teaspoon freshly ground black pepper, 4-6 drops Tabasco sauce. Stir well.

Following pages: Oysters on the Half-Shell

Salade Frisée

A great classic from the more Alpine areas of France and Belgium, this salad must be served as soon as it's made. The combination of the slightly bitter greens with the unctuous dressing makes for a deeply satisfying appetizer.

2 heads curly chicory, rinsed and dried
1/4 pound country-cured, smoked bacon, in 1/4-inch cubes
1/3 cup mild wine vinegar
1-2 teaspoons Dijon mustard (optional)
1 teaspoon freshly ground black pepper

Tear the chicory into reasonably bite-sized pieces in a large salad bowl.

Place the bacon in a large skillet and cook over moderate heat until the fat has rendered out and the bacon bits are starting to get browned and slightly crisp. Take the skillet from the heat and add the vinegar, mustard (if you so choose) and pepper. Let it bubble for a moment and pour it over the chicory. Toss well and serve immediately. Serves 4-6 (depending on appetites).

This salad, along with some good cheese and bread makes a satisfying, rustic lunch or light supper.

Right: Salade Frisée

Prosciutto and Melon

One of the very best summer appetizers is prosciutto and melon. Although domestic prosciutto, especially that made by Volpe, is good, the genuine article from Italy is without compare. It is expensive, but a little goes a long way. By the way, genuine prosciutto is *not* smoked.

1 melon (cantaloupe, honeydew or casaba), dead ripe
1/4 pound prosciutto, sliced as thinly as possible
freshly ground black pepper

Cut the melon in wedges and remove the seeds. Peel each segment and place on a salad plate. Drape slices of prosciutto over each wedge of melon and serve with a pepper mill at hand. Serves 4-6.

Preceding pages: Prosciutto and Melon

Stuffed Mushrooms

1 pound large mushrooms
1 10-ounce package frozen chopped spinach
2 tablespoons olive oil
1 clove garlic, peeled and chopped
1/4 cup grated Parmesan cheese
1 teaspoon black pepper
1/2 teaspoon salt

Remove the stems from the mushrooms. Chop the stems finely.

Defrost the spinach and press as much moisture as possible from them.

In a skillet, sauté the garlic in the olive oil. Add the chopped mushrooms stems and continue cooking until the mushrooms give out some liquid. Add the spinach and heat through until no droplets of moisture appear. Remove from heat.

Mix the cheese with the mushroom-spinach mixture and mound the mixture into the upturned mushroom caps. Arrange on a baking sheet and pour a little olive oil over each. Bake in a 400 degree F. oven until the caps are cooked through and everything is piping hot. Serves 4-6.

Following page: Stuffed Mushrooms

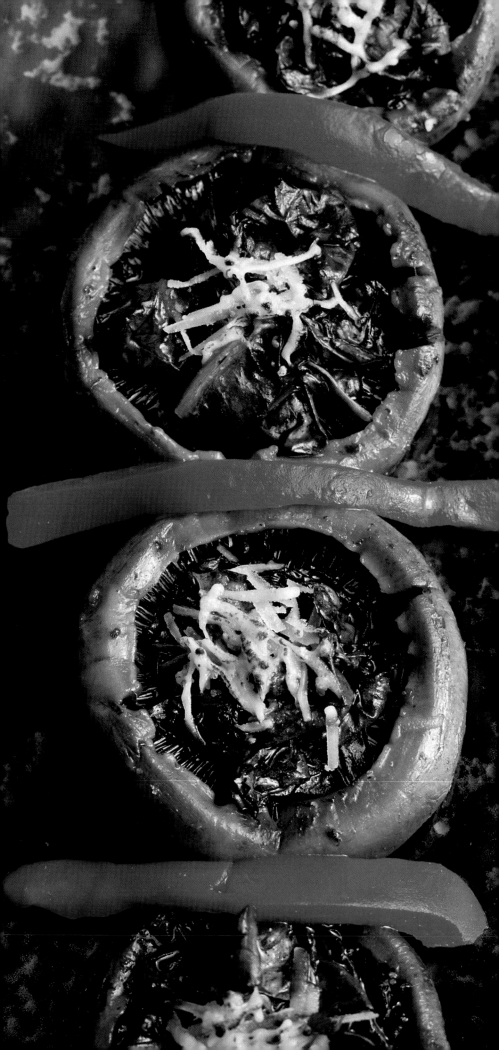

Orange, Onion and Endive Salad

Goes particularly well before roast pork or duck.

4 oranges
1 large, sweet red onion
4 Belgian endives
1/2 cup extra virgin olive oil
juice of 1 orange
1 teaspoon powdered ginger
1/2 teaspoon black pepper
salt to taste

Separate the endives into spears and arrange in a circular
pattern on a large, flat dish.

Peel the oranges, cut in slices and remove pips and pith.
Arrange in overlapping circles on top of the endive

Peel and slice the onion thinly and scatter over the
oranges.

Combine the olive oil, orange juice, ginger, pepper and
salt in a jar and shake to blend.

Pour the dressing over the salad. This tastes best if
served at room temperature. Serves 4.

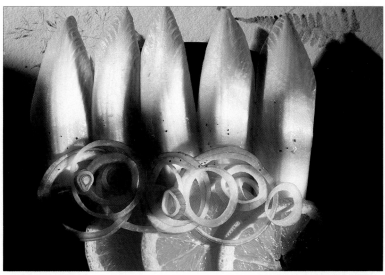

Orange, Onion and Endive Salad

Salami and Olives

One of the simplest and nicest appetizers is a plate of really good salami accompanied by oil-cured or salt-brined ripe (black) olives. To be really good, the salami must be of the best quality obtainable—meaning imported Italian—and the olives should be small, glistening and intensely flavored.

Simply peel the rind from the salami and slice as thinly as possible. Arrange in overlapping circles on a large, flat plate. In the center, place a mound of olives. Accompanied by crusty bread and butter and a glass of cool wine, this is a perfect beginning for a simple dinner or a barbecue.

Preceding pages: Salami and Olives

Grilled Porcini Mushrooms

Porcini are the large—sometimes very much so—Italian mushrooms rich with the flavors of the woods. They can be purchased at specialty greengrocers and some gourmet food shops. Make sure they are fresh.

2 tablespoons extra virgin olive oil
1 clove garlic, peeled and chopped
1 pound porcini
1 tablespoon chives, finely chopped
1/4 cup prosciutto, finely chopped or cubed
1/2 cup Marsala

In a skillet, sauté the garlic in the olive oil. Add the porcini, cut into 1/4-inch strips and cook over medium heat for 10 minutes, stirring now and then. Remove to 4 salad plates.

Add the chives and prosciutto to the pan and heat for 2 minutes. Now add the Marsala and cook over high heat for 3-4 minutes until the sauce has thickened slightly. Spoon equal portions over the porcini and serve at once. Serves 4.

Following pages: Grilled Porcini Mushrooms

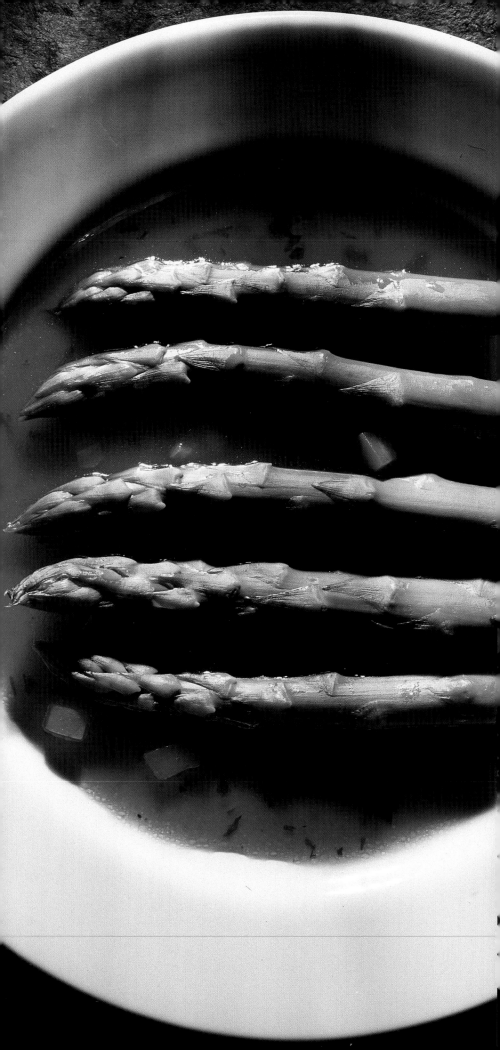

Asparagus Vinaigrette

2 pounds asparagus
3/4 cup extra virgin olive oil
2 tablespoons wine vinegar
1 tablespoon grainy Dijon mustard
1 clove garlic, peeled and finely chopped
1/2 teaspoon black pepper
1 tablespoon pimento, chopped

Clean the asparagus. If they are large, peel the stalks with a potato peeler and cut off the white and woody ends. Lay them evenly in a large skillet and add water to a depth of 1/2-inch. Sprinkle with 1 teaspoon salt. Cover the pot and steam them over medium heat until just tender. Drain and let cool.

Combine the olive oil, vinegar, mustard, garlic, pepper and pimento in a jar and shake well to blend.

Arrange the asparagus spears on 6 individual salad plates and spoon equal amounts of the dressing over each. Serves 6.

Left: Asparagus Vinaigrette

Tricolor Salad

1 bunch arugula
1 head radicchio
1 head Boston lettuce
1 / 2 cup extra virgin olive oil
2 tablespoons wine vinegar
1 teaspoon fresh basil, finely chopped
1 / 2 teaspoon capers, chopped
salt and pepper to taste

Wash and dry the arugula, radicchio and Boston lettuce. Cut off the tough stems of the arugula, and tear all into large, bite-sized pieces.

Combine the olive oil, vinegar, basil, capers and salt and pepper to taste in a jar and shake to blend. Toss with the salad. Serves 4.

Right: The ingredients for a Tricolor Salad—top left, letuce; top right, olive oil; center left, radicchio; center, peppercorns; bottom left, wine vinegar; bottom right, arugula.

Javanese Pork Satés

1/4 cup peanut butter
1 1/2 teaspoons ground coriander
1 teaspoon salt
1/2 teaspoon cayenne
1 teaspoon ground cumin
4 medium onions, chopped
freshly ground black pepper
2 cloves garlic, minced
1 1/2 tablespoons lemon juice
1 tablespoon brown sugar
3 tablespoons dark soy sauce
2 pounds boneless pork, cut in 1 1/2-inch cubes

Mix together all ingredients except for the pork. Add pork cubes and mix together to coat all pieces thoroughly. Cover and refrigerate at least four hours. Thread meat on skewers and grill or broil for 20-25 minutes, turning frequently, and basting with any excess marinade, until crusty brown on all sides.

The meat can also be cut into smaller 3/4-inch cubes, threaded on smaller skewers, and served as an appetizer or as an accompaniment to drinks. Makes 6 servings as a main course, 12 servings as an appetizer.

Preceding pages: Javanese Pork Satés

Smoked Salmon Roll-Ups

1 cup soft herbed cream cheese
12 long, thin-cut slices smoked salmon
capers

Bring the cream cheese to room temperature.
    Place the salmon slices on a plate and spread evenly
with the cream cheese. Roll up and secure with a toothpick
if necessary. Garnish with capers. Serves 12.

Following pages: Smoked Salmon Roll-Ups

Stuffed Potatoes

12 *small red potatoes*
1/2 cup caviar
1/2 cup sour cream or plan yogurt

Boil the potatoes until tender, approximately 8-10 minutes.
Drain and rinse in cold water.

    With a small spoon or melon-baller scoop out a small
amount of the potato. Fill scoop with small amounts of the
caviar and sour cream. Arrange on a platter and serve.
Serves 6.

Stuffed Potatoes

Mussels Marinara

2 pounds mussels
1 onion, finely chopped
1 can imported Italian tomatoes, drained
1/2 cup parsley, chopped
Black pepper
1-2 cups dry white wine

Scrub the mussels and remove the beards.

Place the mussels in a large pot and add the onions, tomatoes, parsley, pepper and wine. Cover and steam over medium heat until the mussels open.

Remove the mussels, with their shells, to a large serving bowl and cover with the liquid. Serve with crusty bread. Serves 4.

Follwoing page: Mussels Marinara

Shrimp Rémoulade

1 large onion, sliced
1 clove of garlic
salt
2 pounds medium shrimp, cleaned and deveined
Rémoulade:
> *1 cup mayonnaise*
> *1 tablespoon capers, chopped*
> *2 teaspoons mustard*
> *1 teaspoon tarragon*
> *1 tablespoon drained mustard or cucumber pickle, finely chopped.*

In a large pot combine the onion, garlic and salt, bring to the boil. Add the shrimp and simmer for 5 minutes or until just pink. Drain and chill.

Combine all the ingredients for the rémoulade in a small bowl. Chill.

When ready to serve, arrange the shrimp on small plates and top with a dollop of the sauce. Serves 6.

Following pages: Shrimp Rémoulade

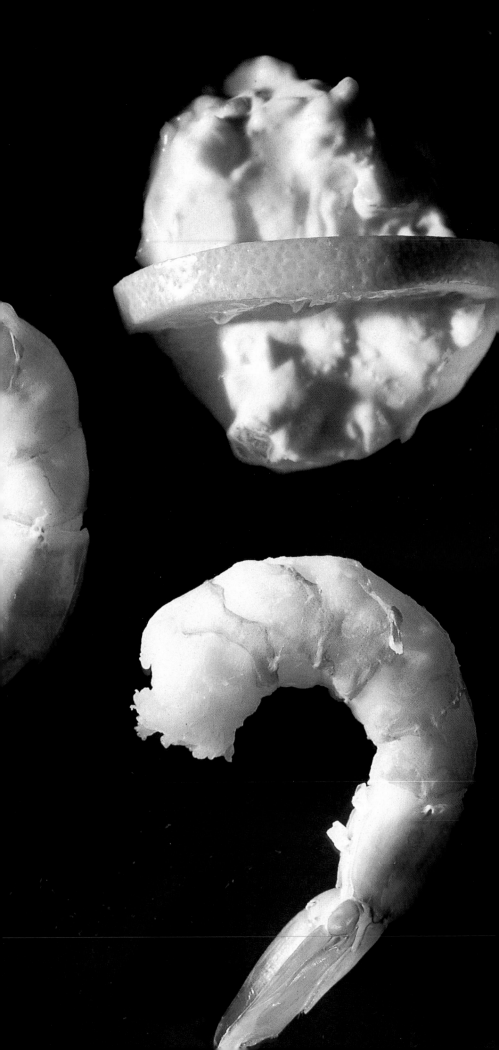

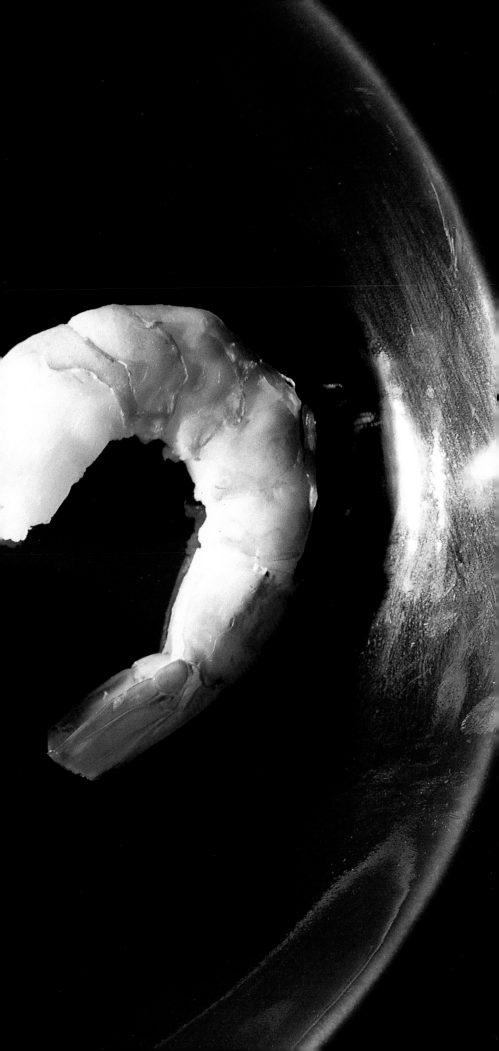

Baked Clams

30 small clams
10 slices of bacon, sliced into 30 pieces
2 tablespoons olive oil
2 tablespoons sweet butter
2 clove of garlic, chopped
2 tablespoons chopped pimento
1 teaspoon dried oregano
1/2 cup unflavored bread crumbs

Preheat the oven to 425 degrees F.

Clean the clams thoroughly and open them. Toss the top shells and pour off some of the liquid. Arrange the clams on a baking sheet.

In a skillet heat the olive oil and butter. Add the garlic, pimento, oregano and bread crumbs. Stir until well mixed. Remove from the heat.

Spoon some of the mixture over each clam and cover with a piece of bacon. Bake for 10-12 minutes or until the bacon is crisp. Serves 6.

Right: Baked Clams

Mixed Salad

Everyone makes a mixed salad, but most are soggy and dull. The most important thing to remember is that greens must be fresh and crisp, additions should be discreet and not watery—this leaves out tomatoes, but they will destroy the balance of a mixed salad faster than anything else—and that the dressing should be light on vinegar. Nothing kills the taste buds faster than an overdose of vinegar.

For the salad pictured here you need:

1 head Boston lettuce
2 bunches of arugula or 2 heads of Belgian endive
1/2 cucumber, preferably Japanese
1 red onion
1/2 cup oil-cured black olives
3/4 cup extra virgin olive oil
3 tablespoons mild wine vinegar
1 clove garlic, peeled and finely chopped
2 teaspoons mustard
        or
2 teaspoons fresh herbs, either basil, tarragon, chervil or oregano
salt and pepper to taste

Clean the lettuces, dry thoroughly and tear into bite-sized pieces. Peel and finely slice the cucumber. If it is the ordinary garden variety, salt it lightly in a colander and let drain for 1 hour. If it's the Japanese variety, it can be used as is. Peel and slice the red onion. Combine all of these in a large salad bowl, add the olives.

Combine the olive oil, vinegar, garlic, mustard or herbs and salt and pepper to taste. Blend well and pour over the salad. Toss well and serve at once. Serves 4-6.

Left: Ingredients for a Mixed Salad

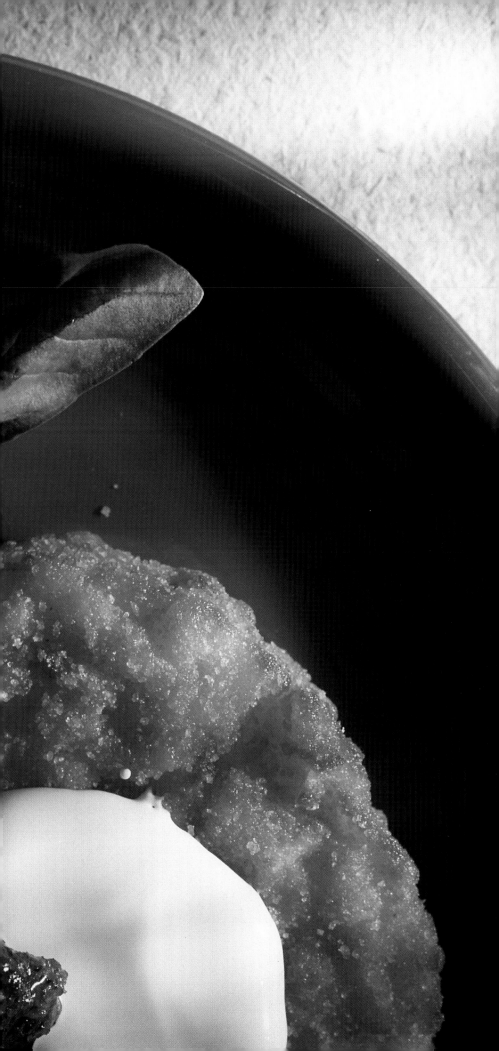

Potato Pancakes with Pesto

A very substantial first course, but perfect before a grilled fish or veal scallops.

1 pound potatoes
1 large onion
2 eggs
salt and pepper to taste
2 tablespoons butter and 2 tablespoons oil
1 cup crème fraiche or sour cream
1/2 cup pesto (see below)

Peel the potatoes and grate them—either by hand or in a food processor. Immediately place the pulp in a strainer and wash thoroughly to get rid of excess starch. Add the grated onion and the eggs and stir thoroughly.

In a large skillet, melt the butter and oil together. Add the potato mixture by the spoonful (a dessert spoon is perfect), making sure they are separated. You will probably have to do the pancakes in batches. Cook them until dark, golden brown, turning once. Drain on kitchen towels, and keep warm in a low oven.

When ready to serve, arrange three on each plate and top with a spoonful each of crème fraiche and pesto.

Pesto
1 bunch fresh basil
1/2 cup pine nuts
2 cloves garlic, peeled
1/2 cup grated Parmesan or Romano cheese
1/2+ cup olive oil

Wash the basil and strip the leaves from the stalks. Place the basil leaves, pine nuts, garlic and cheese in the bowl of a food processor. Pulsing, slowly add the oil until you have a thick paste. You may need more or less than a 1/2 cup depending on the amount of basil and the water content of the cheese. Pesto will keep in a covered container in the refrigerator for 1 week. It can also be frozen, providing you leave out the cheese.

Preceding pages: Potato Pancakes with Pesto

Stuffed Mussels

A middle eastern dish and an especially savory appetizer.

36 large mussels
1 small onion, peeled and finely chopped
3 tablespoons sesame oil
1 cup cooked long grain rice
3 tablespoons currants
2 tablespoons pine nuts
1/2 teaspoon ground coriander
1/2 teaspoon ground ginger
1/2 teaspoon black pepper
2 teaspoons sugar
lemon wedges

Clean and scrub the mussels. Place in a covered saucepan with 1 cup of water and bring to a boil. Cook, covered, until the mussels open. Drain and set aside.

Sauté the onion in the sesame oil until light golden. Add the rice and cook gently until lightly colored. Now add the currants, pine nuts, coriander, ginger, pepper and sugar. Cover the pan and simmer for 5 minutes.

Place a spoonful of the rice mixture into each mussel and close the shells. Serve at room temperature with lemon wedges. Serves 6.

Following pages: Stuffed Mussels

Tortellini Salad

1 / 4 pound prosciutto, shredded
1 cup fresh raw peas
1 tablespoon chopped pimento
3 / 4 cup extra virgin olive oil
2 tablespoon wine vinegar
2 teaspoons Dijon mustard
salt and pepper to taste
1 pound cheese tortellini, cooked and drained

Toss the prosciutto with the peas, pimento, olive oil, vinegar mustard and salt and pepper to taste.

   Add the tortellini and toss well. Serve at room temperature. Serves 6.

Ceviche of Scallops

A ceviche (or seviche) is a dish of raw fish marinated or "cooked" in citrus juice. It's both tasty and healthy.

1 pound bay scallops
1 sweet onion, peeled and finely chopped
1 red pepper, peeled, seeded and chopped
1 yellow pepper, peeled, seeded and chopped
1 cup fresh lime juice
salt and pepper to taste

Combine all the ingredients in a china or glass bowl. Cover and chill for 2–3 hours. Serves 4.

Left: Tortellini Salad

Following pages: Ceviche of Scallops

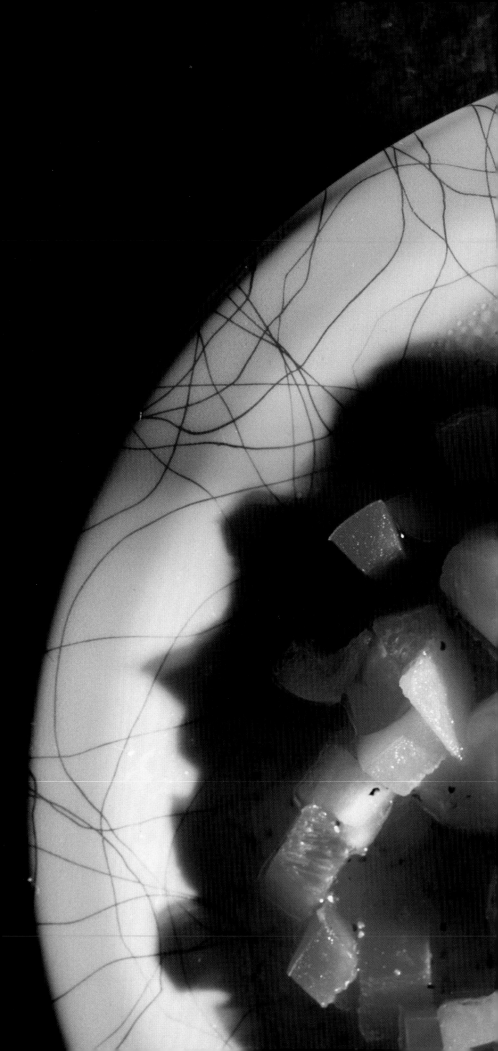

Deviled Eggs

Nothing could be as common as deviled eggs and nothing is so rarely served as an appetizer. This one's special.

8 eggs, hard boiled
1 tablespoon onion, finely chopped
1/4 cup mayonnaise
1/2 teaspoon cayenne pepper
1 tablespoon dry Madeira
4 romaine lettuce leaves
1 tablespoon chives, chopped

Cut the eggs in half lengthwise and scoop out the yolks into a bowl.

Mash the yolks with the onion, mayonnaise, cayenne pepper and Madeira.

Stuff the mixture back into the whites and place 4 halves on a leaf of romaine on 4 salad plates. Garnish with chopped chives. Serves 4.

Right: Deviled Eggs

Tapenade

This spread gets its name from the Provençal word for capers.

1 cup pitted, black, oil-cured olives
1 small can anchovy fillets, drained
1 3 1/2-ounce can tuna in oil
2 cloves garlic, peeled and chopped
2 tablespoons capers, rinsed
1/2 teaspoon black pepper
1 tablespoon brandy

Combine all ingredients in a food processor bowl and process for 1 minute. Let sit at room temperature for 1 hour to blend flavors. Serve with toasted slices of French bread and a strong white wine.

Left: Tapenade and Peasant Bread

Chicken Liver Skewers

1 pound chicken livers
1/4 pound mushrooms
1/2 cup olive oil
1/4 cup lemon juice
1/2 teaspoon ground coriander
1/2 teaspoon black pepper

Marinate the chicken livers and mushrooms in the olive oil and lemon juice mixed with the coriander and pepper for 1 hour.

Thread the livers and mushrooms, cut in piece if too large onto small skewers and broil for 5 minutes turning frequently, until crisp outside and still pink within. Serves 6.

Preceding pages: Chicken Liver Skewers

Steak Tartare

Oddly enough, raw beef—if it's of top quality—can be an excellent appetizer, either alone or as the topping for canapés.

3/4 pound raw beef fillet, ground
1 tablespoon capers
1/2 cup onion, chopped
4 raw egg yolks*

Divide the ground beef into 4 portions. Place each on a plate and sprinkle with capers and raw onion. Make a small depression in each portion and break an egg yolk into it. Each diner mixes his or her own. Pass the pepper mill separately. Serves 4.

*Raw eggs can carry salmonella. Unless you are sure of your sources, do not use raw egg, even though it's traditional. A dollop of plain yogurt will approximate the effect, though the taste will be sharper. It adds the necessary moisture however.

Following pages: Steak Tartare

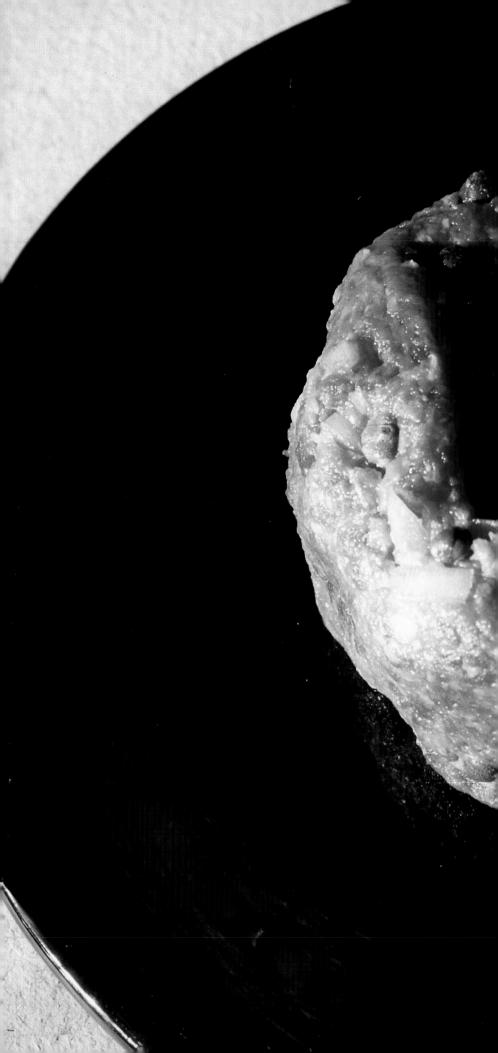

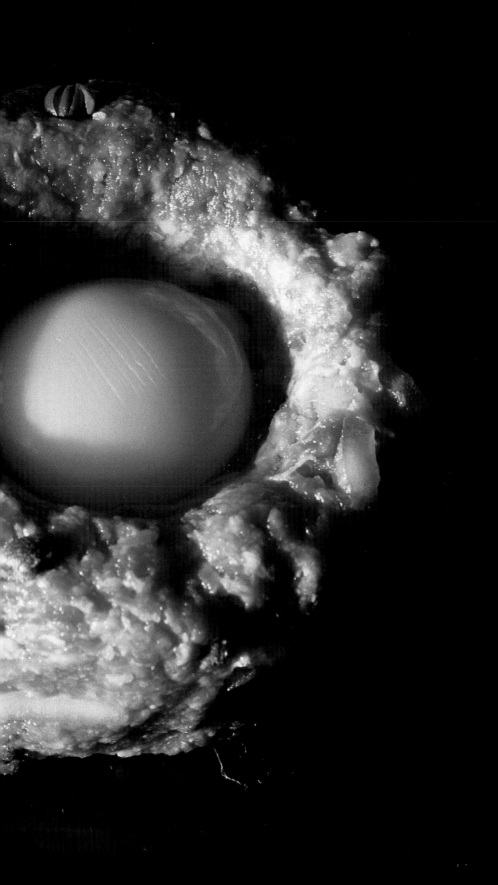

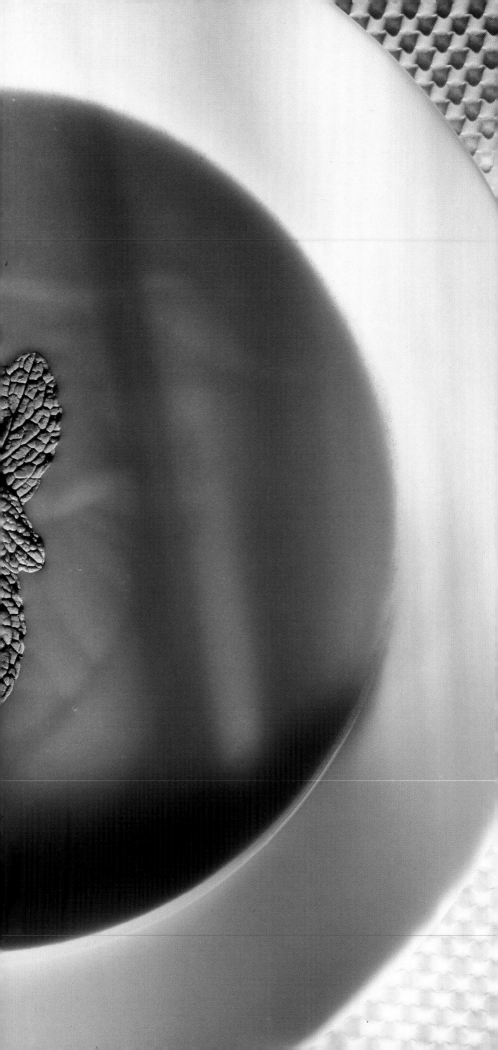

Tomato Soup

Tomato soup made from a can and made from scratch are two entirely different things.

1 1/2 pounds ripe tomatoes, peeled and seeded
1 small onion, peeled and sliced
1 tablespoon fresh basil, chopped
salt and pepper to taste
2 tablespoons butter
1 cup cream, optional

Combine the tomatoes, onion, basil, salt and pepper in the bowl of a food processor. Process for 1 minute.

Melt the butter in a large saucepan. Add the tomato mixture and simmer for 10 minutes.

If desired 1 cup of cream can be added to make this cream of tomato soup. Or olive oil can be used instead of butter (omit the cream) and the soup can be served cold. Serves 4-6.

Left: Tomato Soup

Herring Salad

1 cup pickled herring, cubed
1 cup boiled potatoes, cubed
1/2 cup cooked beets, cubed
1 small onion, peeled and finely chopped
1/3 cup olive oil
1 tablespoon lemon juice
1 tablespoon fresh dill, chopped
salt and pepper to taste

Combine all the ingredients in a mixing bowl and toss well. Serve in mounds on salad plates with pumpernickel and sweet butter. Serves 4.

Variation: leave the herring and vegetables in larger pieces, arrange as in the photo and serve the dressing separately.

Preceding pages: Herring Salad

Yogurt-Cucumber Soup

4 cups plain yogurt
1 cup water
1 cucumber, peeled, seeded and chopped
1 teaspoon dried mint
1/2 teaspoon black pepper
1 tablespoon fresh ginger, grated

Combine the yogurt and water and mix well. Add the cucumber, mint and pepper. Chill well.

When ready to serve, ladle into 4 soup bowls and sprinkle with grated ginger. Serves 4.

Yogurt-Cucumber Soup

Rice Salad

1 cup long-grain rice
2 tablespoons pimento in strips
1 small onion, peeled and chopped
2/3 cup extra virgin olive oil
3 tablespoons lemon juice
2 teaspoons fresh tarragon, finely chopped
salt and pepper to taste
1/4 cup toasted almonds
1 cup small cooked shrimp

Boil the rice in plenty of salted water until still slightly firm.
Drain.

Combine the hot rice with the pimento, onion, olive oil,
lemon juice, tarragon and salt and pepper to taste. Toss
well and let cool.

Before serving arrange the shrimp and almonds over
the heaped up rice. Serves 4-6.

Preceding pages: Rice Salad

Pork Paté

1 pound loin of pork, ground
1/2 pound calf's liver, ground
1/2 pound fatback or salt pork, ground
2 tablespoons brandy
1/3 cup dry white wine
1 clove garlic, peeled and chopped
1 teaspoon black pepper
1/2 teaspoon juniper berries, crushed
1/2 teaspoon nutmeg
4 slices fat bacon

Combine the pork, liver, fatback or salt pork (incidentally, if you use salt pork, no further salt is necessary), brandy, white wine, garlic, pepper, juniper berries and nutmeg in a large mixing bowl. Mix thoroughly and let stand a couple of hours for the flavors to meld.

Mold into a loaf or place the mixture in a small loaf pan. Drape the bacon slices over and cook in a 300 degree F. oven for 1 1/2 hours.

Remove from the oven and leave to cool. Then cover the top with foil or wax paper and weigh down with a couple of cans for 3–4 hours.

Serve thinly sliced with gerkhins and good bread.
Serves 6-8.

Following pages: Pork Paté

Minestrone

2 medium onions, chopped
2 carrots, sliced
2 stalks of celery, chopped
2 potatoes, peeled and chopped
2 zucchini, chopped
1 fennel stem, chopped
1/2 cup fresh peas
1/2 green beans, chopped
1 cup cabbage, coarsely chopped
4 cloves of garlic, chopped
1/2 cup olive oil
1 large can Italian tomatoes
6 cups chicken or beef broth
2-3 cups water
1 cup wine (white or red depending upon broth used)
salt to taste
pepper to taste
1 cup cooked chickpeas
1/2 cup chopped parsley
parmesan cheese for grating

In a large saucepan heat the oil. Add the onions, carrots, celery, potatoes, fennel, zucchini, peas, green beans, cabbage and garlic, cook stirring constantly until vegetables begin to wilt.

Add the tomatoes, broth, water, wine, salt and pepper to taste. Cover and cook slowly for 2–2 1/2 hours. Add the chickpeas, and parsley, and continue cooking without the cover until all the vegetables are tender. Sprinkle with grated Parmesan cheese before serving. Serves 12–14.

Preceding pages: Minestrone

Black Bean Soup

2 cups black beans
1/4 cup sweet butter
2 large white onions, coarsely chopped
3 cloves of garlic, crushed
4–6 scallions, coarsely chopped
1 ham bone with meat attached
salt to taste
pepper to taste
4–6 quarts water
1/3 cup Madeira or port (optional)

Allow the beans to soak overnight in a covered pot of cold water.

In a very large soup or stock pot, melt the butter. Add the onions, garlic and scallions, season with salt and pepper and cook over a medium heat for 3–4 minutes.

Add the ham bone and cook carefully for additional 3 minutes. Add the 4 cups of the water and allow the mixture to come the boil. Lower the heat and simmer very slowly for 7-8 hours. Be sure to leave a small space between the cover and the pot.

Drain and add the beans, simmer the soup for 1 1/2–2 hours longer. If the mixture becomes to thick, add more water. When the soup has cooked for at least 1 hour, add the Madeira or port. Continue cooking until all the ingredients are tender and the soup is thick. Serves 12–14.

Following pages: Black Bean Soup

Stuffed Vine Leaves

1 large jar preserved vine (grape) leaves
3/4 cup long-grain rice
1/2 pound ground lamb
1 large tomato, chopped
1 medium onion, chopped
salt to taste
pepper to taste
2 cloves of garlic, thinly sliced
1 lemon, cut in half
1/3–2/3 cup water

Vine leaves that have been preserved in brine should be soaked in boiling water for 25 minutes and then refreshed in cold water and drained. If you are using fresh vine leaves, they only need to be softened in boiling water.

Soak the rice in boiling water for 5 minutes and then rinse in cold water, drain. Combine the rice, ground lamb, tomato, onion, salt and pepper.

To begin, place one leaf on a working surface with the vein side up. Place a large teaspoon of the rice mixture in the center of the leaf near the bottom stem. Roll up from the bottom and fold both side in. Continue in this manner until all the filling is used.

Place 2–3 of the left over vine leaves on the bottom of a large saucepan. Add the stuffed vine leaves, packed tightly and sprinkle with the garlic and lemon juice. Add at least 1/3 cup of water and weight the leaves with a plate and cover the pot.

Cook for 1 1/2–2 hours or until the leaves are tender. Carefully transfer to a platter and serve. Serves 10.

Right: Stuffed Vine Leaves

Salmon Mousse

2 1/2 teaspoons gelatin
2 tablespoons cold water
2 egg yolks
2 tablespoons sweet butter
1 1/4 teaspoons flour
1 teaspoon salt
1/2 teaspoon curry powder
1 teaspoon Dijon mustard
1 tablespoon lemon juice
3 tablespoons milk
1 1/2 cups cooked salmon, packed

Sprinkle the gelatin into the cold water, set aside.

In the top of a double boiler, over hot, not boiling water, combine the egg yolks, butter, flour, salt, curry powder, mustard, lemon juice and milk. Cook until the mixture begins to thicken. Add the gelatin and stir well. Chill.

Generously grease a ring mold. When the gelatin mixture is almost set, place some of it in the bottom of the mold and then top with the fish. Continue this until ingredients are finished, being sure to end with the gelatin mixture. Chill until firm. Unmold onto a serving plate. Serves 6.

Left: Salmon Mousse

About the Author

Judi Olstein has been a professional baker and food re-
searcher. She is the author of *American Family Cooking*,
The New International Cuisine, *The Great American Baking Book*,
Juicing!, *The Peanut Butter Cookbook* and *The Turkey Cookbook*,
as well as four other books in this series (see back cover).
She lives, and cooks, with her husband in Hoboken,
New Jersey and New Suffolk, New York.